Advanced BLACK BELT LIBRARIANS

Answers to the Questions Librarians Always Ask Me

Warren Davis Graham, Jr.

PURE HEART PRESS
Main Street Rag Publishing Company
Charlotte, North Carolina

*The opinions expressed in this book are my own
and do not necessarily reflect those of any previous
or current employer of mine. But they should.*

Library of Congress Control Number: 2010923419

ISBN: 978-1-59948-240-8

Produced in the United States of America

Pure Heart Press
Main Street Rag Publishing Company
PO Box 690100
Charlotte, NC 28227
www.MainStreetRag.com

For all the librarians and library staff around the world who found my first book useful and have honored me with their friendship. I have endless respect for the patience and professionalism you exhibit in your quest to provide the knowledge of the world to the patron.

Contents

Introduction

This book is a direct result of the overwhelmingly positive response I enjoyed to my first effort, "Black Belt Librarians." I decided to attempt to reach out a little more to everyone by addressing the most common questions I am asked as I travel. The questions really do always stay basically the same, no matter the size of the respective library system or the area of the world.

This took me longer to complete than I had planned, but in three years I was in over 150 libraries and gave over twice as many presentations. I have greatly enjoyed my travels, but at times I have been just exhausted!

Little did I know where things would lead my first day on the job at the Public Library of Charlotte and Mecklenburg County back in 1989. "What could really happen in here?" I silently asked myself as I was given a tour of the main library. Could they really be having the level of problems that was being described to me? Or was I simply working with a bunch of frightened librarians who were afraid of their own shadows?

To my genuine surprise, it was soon evident that the former was indeed the case. On the library's grand re-opening day, after the building had been closed for two years of renovation, I can honestly say I was astounded at the situations I encountered. Intermingled with the majority of patrons, who were there for all the right reasons and enjoying the facility, were a mix of behavior problems than ran the gamut from the innocuous to the insane.

There were people who apparently had waited patiently for the previous 24 months to take a bath in our restrooms. Someone actually asked me if he could rent a shower. Many children ran rampant like baby cheetahs, and it was their oblivious parents who were at fault. More than a few thought this was a new library in every sense and thus they owed nothing for lost books or fines. A few perverts experimented with developing new techniques of staring through the stacks at female patrons. One fine fellow actually had a small mirror duct taped to the top of his shoe to facilitate looking up skirts, but only of patrons who were at least 50 years of age! And to round it all off, there was a good dose of genuinely disturbed people who had nowhere else to go and nothing else to do but come visit us. One fellow had a briefcase full of metal washers. He just wanted to sit at a table and see how high he could stack them and he told everyone in no uncertain terms to stay away from him.

A few years later, a librarian called the director who had hired me, Robert Cannon. She had a problem. A speaker on security had cancelled out at the last minute on a talk he was to give at the PLA conference in Atlanta, and the caller wanted to know if Bob was aware of anyone who could fill in. In a very short three days, I was standing in front of a couple thousand librarians, literally crammed into a ballroom, presenting my first talk on the subject of day-to-day safety in the library.

That's how my second career started and since that day I have traveled the nation, training thousands of library staff. I always thought my home state of North Carolina had some rural areas, but I have visited some *extremely* remote library locations.

In one presentation out west, I was describing how one should go about calling 911 to solicit the best response. This petite, elderly attendee gently raised her hand and sweetly, but anxiously, asked, "But son, what if you don't have 911?" That was news to this city fellow. I had always thought having access to a 911 emergency response was a given.

Another time I was being driven from library to library by a director who had to stop the car and honk to get the buzzards out of the middle of the road. I had never seen a buzzard and had to ask what they were! I mean, it's not like we were in the desert, and I thought that was the only place buzzards lived.

In another state, we stopped at a convenience store filled with customers, and each and everyone one of them stopped pumping gas, playing video games, buying beer or whatever else they were doing and just stared at me. The cashier actually had her mouth open. "Not from around here are you boy?" a gentleman dressed in overalls but no shirt asked me, as he completed his Slim Jim and Mountain Dew purchase. The dinner of champions.

And I will never forget the first time I traveled to a state far up north (that will remain unnamed here). The south has always had the reputation for having all the good old boys, but I will tell you that I saw more confederate car license plates and stickers on this visit than I had ever seen before at home! Quite the eye opener.

You name it. Go ahead, name it. I have more than likely either heard or personally witnessed – on my own or in someone else's library. On the very serious end of things, I responded to a police call at one of our branches early in morning just a couple of months before I retired. The landscaping crew for a neighboring building discovered a body lying on the steps of an outside story time area, located just by our children's area. Tragically, a 21 year old had committed suicide by shooting himself. Worse than the terrible effects of the bullet was the sight of such a young person who had given up before his life really began. I will never forget how much that affected me.

On the opposite end of the spectrum, during the late afternoon of the very same day, back at the main library, I was called to the computer area. A woman had screamed "Fire!" several times and was acting erratically. It turned out that she felt she was not receiving the level of help with her computer that she expected and had yelled to get some attention. Of course, the attention she received from me was not quite what she had in mind.

I think that was the day I decided to leave and did so soon after in August of 2006. After 25 years in security work, I was simply weary of it all and realized that I had been for several years. I was ready to help others learn how to handle these situations and the demand for me to come and train staff was higher than ever.

After traveling constantly ever since (only stopping for six weeks for the birth of my son) and feeling fulfilled by the overwhelmingly positive response to what I had to say, I can say that I definitely made the right decision. I have enjoyed it so much that I can honestly say I have not worked a day since I left the library. This subject of library security still energizes and fascinates me.

This marks my 20th anniversary in the library world. I may not be a librarian, but I think I understand your world quite well. I want you to be safe and I want to help you see the best way of accomplishing that.

This book is meant to be a companion to my first, *Black Belt Librarians*. I would recommend you read that one first since I have tried my very best not to repeat information that I have already given you. That being said, the two can't help but overlap in some areas. I also get a chance to expound on several points that I only touched upon previously.

I will repeat my warning from *Black Belt Librarians* that I tend to write the way I speak (with occasional destruction of the English language). If you ever attend my seminars you will see that I am known for a down to earth and direct presentation of useful, "real world" facts as I have actually experienced them. I want to give you the same with my books, and all the advice and procedures I have for you is empirical, none is classroom theory or textbook supposition.

Everywhere I go, I gain such a great feeling of efficacy when I can help empower a fellow inhabitant of the "Planet Library" we share. I will always be thankful for the many new and lasting friends I have made over the years. I sincerely hope this little book helps you through your day.

Warren Graham
December 2009

On the Lighter Side

Ok, before you ask me for another top ten list, here you go. Compiled by my security officers and me over the years in a sometimes desperate attempt to find the humor in the midst of what could be very serious duties.

The top ten rejected library marketing phrases:

The Public Library...

...Where the Possessed Go to Mingle!
...A House of Knowledge. Do You Fit?
...Patron Dress Code: Four Tooth Minimum.
...Don't Force Us to Call the Circus!
*...Where There **IS** Such a Thing as a Stupid Question.*
...No, Our Staff Members Do Not Want to Date You.
...Where the Demons Go to Hang Out.
...All the Nuts Are Not in the Nuthouse.
...Yes, We Are a Public Building, But No, You Can't Do Anything You Want.
...We <u>Also</u> Pay Our Salaries!

Now a few more most requested stories from the front lines. Once more unto the breach, dear friends!

My friend was having one heck of a game. He was obviously at the end of the second half and the winning or losing of the game was all on his shoulders. He moved in all directions, constantly dribbling and putting moves on his opponents that left them guarding air. He came down in middle, entered the "paint" and dunked home two points. There was only one problem with this scene. He was in the middle of the reference area all alone and had no basketball.

I went up and asked him to give me his best forward pass, which he did. I challenged him to take it from me and proceeded in an imaginary dribble to the front door. I then gave him back the "ball" and told him he couldn't play basketball in the library because someone could fall and get hurt. He readily agreed and apologized for not thinking of that himself.

He came back the next day just long enough to find me and give me a thumbs up. "The Bobcats (Charlotte's basketball team) picked me up in the first round!" he cheered as he dribbled his imaginary ball out the door. We never saw him again.

I cannot tell you how many times I heard, "But I'm homeless," as if that were a free pass to do anything one wanted in the library. I once heard this from a gentleman who was drinking a huge bottle of wine and eating his fast food chicken dinner, while sitting on and using the toilet.

One fellow was obviously intoxicated and I escorted him to the security office. He didn't have any liquor on him but in his duffle bag, I found two huge bottles of mouthwash and one only had a couple of spoonfuls left. I assumed that he had the mouthwash to cover up the booze he must continually have on his breath. Then I noticed the alcohol content of the mouthwash and realized that was how he was obtaining his buzz!

Over the years I saw people drink all kinds of cologne (the cheaper the better, patrons told me). Glue sniffing stayed popular as well. I began to notice that our automatic deodorizers were seldom working. Eventually I discovered a fellow "huffing" one of the cans that he had taken out of the dispenser to get high… so *that* was what was going on!

One fellow stopped me at the front desk and showed me his huge bottle of olive oil that he swore was an antidote for whatever ailed you. His pupils were dilated and it was obvious he was on something. He proceeded to open the bottle and started talking huge gulps and shouting how great it was. I escorted him out the door.

Lucy the vamp was quite a character. She was only in her 60's but looked a couple of decades older. Strutting around at about 5'2", she always had her "face on," as she put it. In her case that meant so much make-up that she looked like an escapee from the planet Revlon. Of course, she had her hair dyed jet black, which contrasted with her crimson lipstick. I imagine that was her look in the 40's. She told everyone that she lived at the shelter, but my contacts there were not familiar with her.

My first week at the library, Lucy came on strong. She told me flat out that she had an eye out for younger men and that she liked me, and expressed to me in no uncertain terms what she would like to do about it. I must admit that this was one of the few times that I was taken completely off guard and stumbled for what to say. I simply told that while I appreciated the compliment, I didn't have time for that nor did I want to hear that from her again. She looked genuinely shocked and walked out the door. She would always come in and look toward my office, but never tried to say anything like that to me again.

There's the old saying that when you have to go you have to go. At least that is what the woman told me while she was sitting atop a trash can at two o'clock in the middle of a beautiful day right outside the library. She asked me what someone was supposed do when she couldn't find a restroom in uptown.

In her frustration, she had dropped her pants and was using the trashcan as a toilet. Her "business" was complicated so she was reading a magazine to pass the time. The police, much to their joy, had to lead her away.

Trapped in the park bench of doom, a man was yelling for someone to help him. He needed all the help he could get. In a park outside the children's room, we had several benches that were four feet long and were capped by circular arm rests that were about 18 inches in diameter. This fellow had decided to sleep off his intoxicated state by lying lengthwise on the bench. He had put both legs through the far arm rest and somehow, someway, had gotten both of this arms over his head and through the other arm rest. You should see that bench. It was an impossible physical feat, but he had done it. When he awoke, he could not get his arms down and was trapped.

By the time I arrived at the request of the children's staff, I found about 20 kids looking out the window in amazement and watching what the man was going to do next. I saw that he was drunk, so called the police to meet me out in the park.

During his struggle to free himself, his pants had dropped down to his lower hips, exposing him to the world and to the kids. As the police arrived he stated that he had to "take a piss" and that we needed to stand back. With that he relieved himself straight up in the air, not unlike Old Faithful at Yellowstone. While we didn't care for the show, the kids got a big kick out of it and were pointing, yelling and cheering as the police freed the guy and carried him to the police car.

Enter the master of disguise. A white male, about 5'7" and 250 lbs, was banned from the library for being intoxicated and cursing staff. He was dressed in army green camouflage pants and shirt and was accompanied by his companion, a very short black female who was easily as wide as she was tall, with a hot pink snow parka and splayed out hair that suggested a firecracker had gone off in her mouth.

Later in the evening of the day he was banned, he came back with his girlfriend and they were both dressed the same way as earlier, but now he had a ski mask on with only his eyes visible. "You guys are really good," he commented as I lead him to the security office. "How did you recognize me with my mask on?"

One of the most bizarre situations I encountered was over the simplest of matters. A man was using one of our computers when we first opened our computer lab. He was allowing his kid, who was only old enough to crawl, to get under the table and not only go in and out between the other patron's legs, but more dangerously, play with the power strips. He knew what I was going to say when I approached and cut me off by yelling that his child could do whatever he wanted since his father was a taxpayer. No amount of reason could make a difference and it was very awkward for me, but eventually he gave me no choice but to ban him from the building.

I was in the process of dealing with a man who had cut into a 1920 newspaper from our stacks. "I just don't understand why you are making such a big deal out of this," he screamed. "The damn paper is almost a hundred years old!"

While walking through the Popular selection area I noticed a woman sitting and reading quietly at a back table. Something caught my attention, although at first I didn't know what it was. As I stepped over, I noticed the lady had a huge rat on her shoulder. For a moment I thought she was being attacked by the thing, but as I started to say something, I saw her pass a piece of cracker to it. I then saw that the rat had a string around its neck and the other end was attached to the lady's wrist.

I can't describe the conversation we had because it made no sense whatsoever. Let's just say that she could not understand why she couldn't have her pet rat "Mickey" in the library, and I eventually had to have the police help me escort her out and ban her.

A fellow was in administration demanding years of "back rent" from the library. He stated that he had the original lease that he and Andrew Carnegie had agreed on and that he was owed millions of dollars. I told him he would have to return with someone from the Carnegie family, which he readily agreed to and said that would be no problem. The last I saw of him was when he rode away on his little, pink girl's bike.

Every once and a while I got a reminder that I never knew who I might be dealing with and that no one was "harmless" no matter how they looked. A police officer was placing a seemingly hapless gentleman under arrest and I was helping the officer search the man's pockets. In every pocket of his pants, jacket and shirt – even in his shirt breast pocket, we found some type of weapon. He had several box cutters, knives and even a sharpened screw driver; a total of 14 weapons. I couldn't resist the temptation to ask him if he was some type of ninja.

Part One:
For the Front Trenches

"The one sure way to fail is to try to please everyone."
—Bill Cosby

"The truth lies in the simple, but it is sought in the far away."
—Mencius

Question: *"What are the most common design problems you have seen in your travels to libraries?"*

I see the same, basic intrinsic design problems in many libraries. You must watch the process of planning a building carefully, as you do not want to be in the position of having to "fight" it daily. I'm sure many of you have learned this lesson the hard way. Your building should enhance and add to security rather than detracting from it by creating even more problems for the staff.

I would list the problems as follows and in no particular order as they are all equally important:

1—Circulation desks too far from the entrance and/ or book alarm.

2—Teen areas that cannot be seen by staff and/or are not staffed.

3—Computer areas set up where you cannot readily see screens.

4—No doors on staff areas.

5—Bathrooms in vestibule areas where staff cannot see them.

6—Children's areas that have gone overboard with a "play land" environment.

Circulation desks that are too far from the book alarm and/or entrance make it difficult for staff to address a possible theft situation when the alarm sounds. You don't want to have to yell across the room to question someone as that can be awkward not only for you, but for the patron as well. You can easily embarrass someone into a verbal or even physical situation by appearing to come on too strong. And if the patron doesn't respond to your long distance inquiry, it's usually impossible to get over to them expediently, and then they are out the door and long gone.

I cover number two more thoroughly in another question later in the book, but it bears repeating. Every time I have seen a teen area that is not supervised or it cannot be seen clearly by staff, it results in problems. Put it where you can see it. It is not about "trust," it's about a bunch of kids, period. Yes, I know this answer will upset some of the teen librarians I know, but I am asked about this constantly in my travels and simply making the young adult area more visible often immediately makes things more controllable.

If you are going to limit what the patrons can view in your computer area, you should place the computer screens facing a staff desk, so the patron's back is to the staff. This is a huge deterrent. If you were coming in to look at things that you were not supposed to, you would go where no one could easily see the screen. Have filters? Well, they help, but if you think that is stopping everyone from accessing porn sites, you are very mistaken. The same goes for those recessed screens and privacy screens. Those are the computers such users go to first.

And yes, I know that some libraries allow patrons to look at anything they want, but from my experience, those libraries generally have more problems than the libraries that have limitations for the patron.

Staff areas need doors and they need to be locked. Yes, I know this is a pain, as you go through some of these doors a hundred times a day. That's just too bad. Please learn from the countless libraries I have visited that have had problems occasioned by unsecured staff rooms. Staff areas need doors and they need to be locked.

A common design in newer libraries is to have a big vestibule area that entails a meeting room and bathrooms. This is nice and convenient for patrons and usually a nightmare for staff. The staff can't see the restrooms and after an incident, they can't tell who did what or when.

I often visit children's rooms where the staff is crying the blues about parents bringing their kids in and letting them go wild. What they don't realize is that they have often created a play land, in an effort to be "kid friendly," that encourages such behavior. Honestly, if I hadn't worked in a library and had taken my two year old in some of these areas I've seen, I would naturally think that the library wanted my kid to run and play. So you have to watch this. I have seen buildings with unique areas that are quite beautiful and certainly get the child's attention without giving them twenty ways to fall to their doom.

Question: *"What rules should we have?"*

First of all, let me say that for you folks out there who want a rule for everything and a procedure manual that tells you what you need to do in every possible situation, I am going to disappoint you. Such a document is impossible to collate, even though I've known many a staff member who expected that. Every security situation is different to varying degrees and no two incidents are exactly alike. Human interaction is just too dynamic.

The best you can do is first have rules for library use, then establish guidelines on what you usually do when someone breaks them. You cannot have rules without guidelines. That being said, there are always exceptions to any rule, and that is where your thought and discretion applies. Staff needs to understand that ultimately, nothing takes the place of common sense judgment.

I always disliked many of our rules in Charlotte that the board of trustees and our lawyer had decided upon. I thought some of them were unnecessary and others were far too wordy. I think my favorite was *Soliciting for prostitution*. "Wow, where does it say I can't be a hooker in here?"

And do you really need to state that you can't steal from the library? With regard to rules, it should always be about less and not more. I've seen many bizarre rules in my travels, but stating that patrons can't steal is still my favorite.

Causing intentional alarm by indecent exposure was another great one. "Well," I suppose the perpetrator would say, "I didn't *intend* to alarm her; it was just my way of saying hello!"

One rule you should have for sure is a little jewel I came up with several years after I began working at the library. I have since shared this many times with other libraries and they now consistently use it. This is what I was allowed to add to our list of things that were not allowed:

"Any behavior that is disruptive to library use."

Let me explain why this is so great to have in writing as part of your rules and regulations for library use. Let's say you cannot decide when someone smells strongly. I mean the patron that clears out the entire non-fiction area when he enters it. You can argue and debate what is an "offensive odor" all you like, but that patron was certainly "disruptive to library use."

The same applies to the patron who wants to stand at the circulation desk and argue endlessly about fines or some other problem. At times the matter at hand is a dead issue since you have given breaks before or this is a time when no possible exception can be made. You do not have time to keep listening and saying the same thing in reply over and over. Past a certain point, what are they becoming? Yes, they too are being "disruptive to library use," because you have other patrons to help and other duties to complete.

The library needs to know exactly what they want to be to the public and realize the inherent limitations. The libraries that try to be everything to everyone and always say "yes" to the patron are often the ones that have the most problems.

Your rules should be as simple and brief as possible. You should be able to put them on a large, bookmark size card. On the back you should list your policy regarding unattended children. When you change your rules and/or go to this format, always include one of these bookmarks for every patron when they check out. Have a stack of them at the self-checkout for patrons as well. Here is an example on the following page:

(Front of book mark)   *(Back of book mark)*

The library does not allow: **Children in the library:**

Sleeping

Loitering

Disruptive behavior

Food or drink

Soliciting or selling

Misuse of restrooms

Not wearing shoes or shirt

Petitioning/distributing

materials

Excessive number or size bags

(List your policy here on children left unattended or after hours. List both the minimum age children can be left alone and the minimum age of those responsible for watching them.)

Internet Use:
(List what isn't allowed.)

—Failure to comply with the library may result in suspension of library privileges.

—Theft or damage of library materials is a serious offense and may also lead to arrest.

—Trespassers will be prosecuted

These rules are given only as examples and I don't mean to imply that they are applicable to your particular library. Only you can ultimately decide the rules you need, because you are the one who actually works in your library. No one but you can know your clientele and what rules are necessary to control the environment. The location of your library and your usual patrons dictate the rules you need.

My favorite story about unnecessary verbiage comes from the days of World War II. A civil defense pamphlet issued by the government stated that, "Illumination must be extinguished when this premises is vacated." Upon seeing this, President Roosevelt became aggravated and said, "Damn! Why can't they just say turn out the lights when you leave the house?"

Many times in my travels frustrated staff tell me that their library is trying to be everything to everyone. They don't want to tell people "no." They want no trouble of any kind and they don't want to be a "house of correction." But the plain fact is that people cannot do whatever they want in your building, so that requires you to educate the patron as to what you do not allow and there is no getting around that fact.

It equates to this:

1 - You have rules for library use.
2 - Patrons must follow those rules.
3 - If they don't, they can't use the library.

I am often asked about how to actually word the rules. For instance, putting up a sign that says "Please turn off your cell phone," rather that "No cell phones." I understand the well-meaning intention of trying to soften the sound of what is not allowed, but I still think it is better and infinitely more effective to use the most direct manner. Try both examples and you will see that the second version I mentioned is much more effective than asking them to "please" do something. When you start the rule like that, it sounds like a request rather than something that is not allowed.

Making sure your staff is consistent is a much higher priority, and will get you quicker results than endlessly debating how to word the rules. I found that the patrons who needed to be told the rules the most, needed to see them in the most simple and frank manner possible.

Loitering is another issue I am constantly asked about and here is the bottom line based on my observations. People in the library should be using the library. If you let people just come in and hang out for whatever reason, it lends itself to behavior problems. I have found that overall, libraries that require you to be reading, studying, etc. have more control over their environment than the ones that don't.

So, keep your rules simple and clarify your guidelines. Make sure the staff know the rules (you would be amazed at the libraries I have visited where many staff simply do not know what is not allowed in their own building), and make the decision to move ahead with it all. Don't get bogged down trying to create a perfect policy. There is no such thing, and when you discover weaknesses in your procedures, you'll adjust them. After all, security is a living thing and doesn't remain fixed. If you are not careful, you'll end up with policy that is so wishy-washy that it doesn't really say anything.

Question: *"What should be our priority when developing a security plan?"*

Simplicity, along with basic guidelines for the advisement of rules and how you are going to train the staff so everyone can be consistent. I would also add that a firm *commitment* to controlling the library environment is absolutely essential. In other words, consistency, consistency, consistency. There have certainly been some libraries that I have visited that simply do not put up with disruptive behavior, and it's the staff that makes sure of that. I've also seen this in libraries in the same organization that just a few miles apart from one another. One branch was on top of things and the other was seemingly oblivious to everything happening around them and avoiding contact with the patrons if at all possible

I know that it *sounds* good to say that you don't want to "confront patrons" about their behavior and that you don't want to be a "house of correction," and that you want everyone to have a "great library experience" and have a place where patrons can "be themselves," etc. I too wanted to teach the world to sing in perfect harmony. But then you have the guy who follows an employee through the staff door a half hour before you open, goes to a computer and logs on, while knowing full well what he is doing. You approach him and he ignores you or goes off the deep end, maybe even so far as to curse and/or threaten you. What do you do with *him*?

Your plan should aide you in sustaining an environment that is conducive to library use. Period. Look at your existing plan. Does it help you, hinder you or not actually say anything? Or, does it attempt to say too much? In that case you have to be careful that you do not make staff too manual dependent. Enable staff to use their discretion when needed

Front line staff need help. They do not have the staff or the time to keep up some complex system and vacuous procedures with multiple warnings to patrons. The burden should be on the person who will not follow the simple rules of the library, not the staff!

Question: *"We keep reporting problems but administration won't listen. What should we do?"*

First and foremost, make sure that you continue doing all that you *can* do and don't stop trying because of what administration won't let you do. You can still make quite an impact with heightened awareness and staff training. Being consistent in rule advisement and staff communication doesn't cost a dime. You can also still help yourself by documenting various security statistics that I talked about in my first book.

In that example, I combined all three forms (security incident report, daily tally sheet and potential problem log) into one report. To simplify things even more, let me make the following suggestions.

You probably have an incident report already, but just make sure that it is as concise and brief in layout as possible. No one wants nor has time to fill out a four page incident report. You will end up with half the incidents not recorded and that is not going to do you much good. Also, require the incident reports to be submitted within 24 hours while everyone's memory about the situation is fresh and administration can be informed on a timely basis. Remember that you are writing the report for someone who wasn't there, so do not omit pertinent details. Take time to illustrate exactly why a certain action was taken. The report may call for immediate safeguards to be put in place or for existing procedures amended, so don't drag your feet in getting the incident properly recorded.

Then, simply take a sheet of paper and write the date and day at the top. Keep it at the circulation desk. Every time anyone corrects a patron's behavior, make a tally mark. This should be easy since all my librarian friends love to take tallies!

The third thing to is to keep up what I call Potential Problem logs (you can see a version on the next page). This is a simple way of tracking patrons who are acting suspiciously. Or maybe you have corrected someone's behavior and your heightened awareness (that you have acquired since reading my last book) tells you that this patron will probably be someone you will have to deal with again. You can start a log and if you don't have a name, use some moniker that you pass on to your coworkers. Just make sure whatever nick name you make for him does not suggest any bias or is derogative in any way.

POTENTIAL PROBLEM LOG

Subject's Name: _____

Description: _____

_____

Date: _____ **Filled by:** _____

Problem: _____

_____

_____

_____

Date: _____ **Filled by:** _____

Problem: _____

_____

_____

_____

Date: _____ **Filled by:** _____

Problem: _____

_____

_____

_____

Date: _____ **Filled by:** _____

Problem: _____

_____

_____

_____

_____

Now, instead of just telling the boss how busy you are with security, you can *show* him with these three, cumulative totals every month.

Over the years that I was with the library, I had great support from my original director. That doesn't mean that I got everything I wanted security- wise, nor does in mean that we always agreed. On rare occasions (actually I can only remember two), I was overruled on my decisions with a security incident. When that happened, I always simply chalked it up to my boss having an agenda that I was not privy to at my level of management or that from where he sat, his decision seemed best for the library. I didn't let it get in the way of the problems of the current day.

Someone was telling me recently that their director was complaining to him that he was "banning too many people." *If* you have procedures in place and rules for library use, *how can you ban too many*? If you have the unfortunate luck to have to eject, let's say, three people this week, do you stop and give everyone else a free pass just because you fear reprisal of some type? That is exactly the type of inconsistency that will get you in a world of trouble.

If the patron's behavior gets him ejected, the onus is on him and not the library. Why do libraries see themselves as the bad guys when someone will not abide by the simple rules of library use? If the next ten people who are ejected are bank vice presidents for example, then that's just the way it happened. The the same goes if they are street people or teachers or wealthy or whatever. *You take them as they come and treat everybody the same.*

Some folks in the library world go to great lengths trying to explain why they don't want to ban patrons permanently, but it is simply the height of irresponsibility to allow some people back into the building. You can talk about the bad patron's "rights" all day, but what about the "rights" of the good patrons? Don't they have the "right" to a safe library?

Keep in mind that there are five things a "Black Belt" librarian or staff member never does:

1—They never let what they cannot do get in the way of everything they *can* do.

2—They know that they can control their environment. They learn to feel in charge. They do not let the behavior problems dictate the pace of the library.

3—They are problem solvers and are resolved enough to make decisions. They are the "go to" staff. They never waste time by playing the easy role of the critic. Being a constant critic of everything takes no talent. It's so much easier to be critical than correct!

4—They consistently work to simplify and clarify procedures. They do not get caught up in the endless "what if" game.

5—They work to develop and maintain a quiet awareness of their surroundings. They never say that safety and security is someone else's job. Security is everyone's business, period, and they never forget that.

6—They focus on being a real world team so they can be consistent and have each other's backs.

Question: *"I'm so understaffed. How can anyone expect me to also be security in my branch?"*

Stop thinking of "security" as separate issue and understand that it is just a vital part of working in any facility that is open to the public in this day and age. It is just part of the process, like good customer service. Even as a kid in retail, I never thought of customer service as a separate entity from, say, good merchandising; it was just a given that all these elements made up the business and you couldn't have a business if you were missing any one of them.

This question is usually the end result of common problems I see consistently in my travels.

—Lack of guidelines for the enforcement of the rules.

—Lack of consistency in enforcement.

—Lack of stringent ban lengths.

—Lack of administrative support

—Lack of requiring the patron to actually be *using* the library.

Simplify and correct any of the above process in which you may be lacking, and telling a patron what is not allowed in the library will instantly become easier.

Part Two:
The Librarian in the Mirror

**"Truth cannot be perceived until we come to
understand ourselves."
—Bruce Lee**

**"The great artist is the simplifier."
—Amiel**

Question: *"How can I improve my confrontational
skills?"*

Allow me to stop you right there. In the future, please
don't ever think of dealing with a patron who is upset
over something as a "confrontation." It is much the same
with the phrase "conflict resolution." Forget those terms or
you will wind up working against your own viscosity before
you even open your mouth. When you think that way, you
automatically tense yourself and put an unnecessary burden
on your mind.

It's always about communication with the patron, never
confrontation. In my first book, I outlined different emotional

levels that a patron may be in and how best to respond. If you believe and concentrate on your strategy, the natural by-product will be more confidence in your abilities.

For those of you who say you just can't step up and communicate with the patron on this level, I will tell you this: the subconscious has no sense of humor whatsoever. Every single cell in your body is listening to you constantly and whether you tell it you can do this or that you can't. How you talk to yourself is a personal journey indeed, and while others can help you, ultimately only you can know what makes you tick. I can't do that for you. I will add that if I could learn to do this, anyone can and I could not be more sincere when I say that. During my seminars when I say that by nature I am passive, introverted and emotional, I've had many people look at me like I'm being coy just to give them a false sense of confidence, but that is simply not true. Why would I try to mislead you on this when I am trying to help you?

Or some may say that it is easier for me because I am a man. Ladies, are you hearing yourselves? I have taught these techniques to thousands of female library staff and security personnel, and gender usually works in your favor rather than hampers you. Or people assume I have military experience so that helps me have the proper bearing (sorry to disappoint, but I was never in the service). I try to stay in reasonable shape, so some say that makes the difference. And while I believe that doesn't hurt, especially for a security officer, I have seen folks off all shapes and sizes who can project authority. These are skills anyone can learn if they simply work to apply them.

I quote Byron in my last book. He once wrote that "adversity is the first path to truth." How very true that is. When one faces a challenging situation, such a demanding patron, one quickly finds out how self-assured they are under pressure, or how they just fall apart and can't think what to do.

While this subject alone could fill a book, I will just say that first, we must have a willingness to engage. That is to say, we must have the desire to acquire and hone our skill level in this regard. You can have the propensity to be unnerved by the public, and even a general dislike of them. You can be just plain afraid of patrons and still develop an adequate skill level. But you have to apply yourself and be honest with yourself regarding your weaknesses. You can't get a hold of yourself if you don't know what to grab on to. *An ability to develop interpersonal skills starts with first developing and maintaining an inner compatibility.*

I would wager that most people have no idea why in some situations they react without thinking, while in other circumstances they think and respond clearly. When you have to ask yourself, "what was I thinking," more than likely you weren't thinking at all.

When you are fueled by the momentum of mindlessness, you soon become a human doing rather than a human being. You become a sum total of your fear that marches to the rhythm of whatever is happening around you, instead of a being who is aware of, understands and flows with your personal, natural, inner rhythm.

Question: *"How do <u>you</u> keep your cool? Don't you ever get afraid? I am not you and I just can't walk up to someone and tell them that they can't do whatever they are doing that is against the rules!"*

A good friend of mine at work would often ask me the same question regarding my handling of problem patrons. Invariably, he and I would be walking around and discussing some library matter, when I would see a behavior problem and stop to correct it without incident. My friend was always amazed. "How do you do that?" He asked. "How can you just suddenly shift gears like that and then actually get them to listen to you?" It was a great compliment, but I have to admit to you that it was never easy or natural for me; I simply developed a procedure to that helped me become good at it. I had to work on it diligently.

The best way to keep your head in a tense situation is to simply know what you are doing and to have confidence in both your and the library's strategy for dealing with security situations. You may not naturally have self-confidence or you may have the tendency to doubt yourself in these situations, but the next best thing is to have confidence in your *strategies*. You must have a plan of action that you can apply regardless of how you feel physically or emotionally at any give time. That is what made the critical difference for me.

Self-efficacy is a simple formula. It is the natural outcome of consistently applying correct, basic fundamentals and nothing more. It is not complicated, but you do need to learn to focus your mind and stabilize your concentration on your plan.

Question: *"What if I have a staff member who just will not follow security procedures no matter how much I emphasize their importance?"*

I get this question so often that I collated an entire three hour training session that I now present on management and leadership!

I could never understand staff who were given responsibilities and just would not follow through. That just does not compute with me, and not only with regard to security procedures. With some staff, they fall short in most aspects of their work. Others spend more energy avoiding tasks than it would take to actually complete them!

I was asked once in a seminar what to do if one did not agree with policy, didn't think it was the correct way of going about things and did not want to follow the established procedures.

My answer to that is simply that you should follow the stated chain of command to voice your complaints through, making sure you do not skip any levels. If at the end of the process, things do not change to your liking, you can leave and find another job where you can tell administration how to do things your way (good luck) or you can stay and adjust your perspective and do what is required.

Not locking your car doors when driving is one thing, but when you're on the job you simply have a broader responsibility. By not following the libraries security procedures, you not only endanger yourself, but everyone else in the building.

I know that you will experience some resistance to some of your procedures. Staff will go along with changes as long as they are not inconvenienced, and some of your procedures will be inconveniences at first. It's a sacrifice you and your staff must be willing to make.

You can't control who comes in the door, so why wouldn't all your staff want to work within the library to control things internally as much as possible? If everyone would simply try, you will be pleasantly surprised at what all you can accomplish. This is not a complicated matter; just simple, common sense. Every goal is easier if everyone just does their job.

I can teach any employee, but they have to care in the first place. If they don't care about doing the job and if they don't want to help you, there is not much you can do. If you are in the position to do so, cut your losses and move on with documentation, discipline and separation if needed.

I have heard some staff say that they "don't want to be police officers" and I can relate because neither did I, and I wasn't. But having people skills, maintaining awareness and having the willingness to engage is part of working with the public. No matter how you go about a security program, sooner or later, everyone is going to have to get up and go over and tell a patron "no." That's just the way it is, and everyone should be required to do their part.

I was far from a perfect manager, but I had my strengths and I considered one of them to be a simple platform for grading my staff. I always measured them by how they performed in three, separate areas: the physical, the ethical and the attitudinal, or P.E.A. as I call it. Let me explain how this fits into the question at hand.

The physical part of a staff members' jobs is simply the way they handle their assigned day to day duties. How efficient are they with their work?

The ethical part concerns what they do when you, as their supervisor, are not around. Are they trustworthy or are they stealing? Does their productivity fall when they know you are not there? Do they sit if you want them to stand? Do they avoid and ignore patrons?

The attitudinal part is the third equal part of the pie. How do they interact with the patrons and the other staff? How do they respond to your daily instruction, guidance and leadership? Are they team players? Do they help or hinder your goals?

They may be great with productivity and they may keep the quality up when you are not present, but if they are constantly complaining or cannot get along with their coworkers, that can be cause for disciplinary action. Or they may have a great attitude and you trust them implicitly, but they do not do the basic physical tasks you assign.

The same follows if they exceed your expectations with their duties. Everyone likes them and their attitude is always positive, but they cannot be trusted to do the job when you are not immediately supervising them. On your day off, the standard drops. Or, it's certainly an issue if you think they are taking money or collection from the library.

I simply kept a spiral notebook. It had pages for each person that reported to me. I always noted dates and time they did an exceptional job and when I praised them for their efforts. Then I also noted whenever they failed in the areas of the physical, ethical or attitudinal aspects of their duties as well as times I had to offer any counseling or reprimands. These copious, but simple notes were all I ever needed to hold my staff accountable, and I never had any issues or problems if termination was ultimately required.

Part Three:
The Impossible Patron

Student: "People are strange, aren't they?"
Master: "Yes, *we* are."

Question: *"What if my manager won't back me up when I follow the security procedures that the library has put in place?"*

The library world is no different that what I often saw in my previous career in retail management. This was during my early 20's. You had some people who were good salespeople, and dependable, and maybe they even had business degrees. They were hard workers and everyone liked them. Before you knew it, some of these folks would end up as managers or assistant managers, and that is where the problems began. They were great employees, but knew nothing of managing a facility, let alone people.

I was far from being the perfect manager, but over the years I have seen quite enough to know that management is a skill that not everyone can learn.

You have to have the right managers in the right library branches before you can even think of how to control the environment. Managers cannot be in denial about what needs to be done to have a safe library. If a manager thinks, for instance, that the answer to patron problems is to say "yes" to everyone, then you are on the Titanic, my friend, and the ice field is dead ahead! I mean if you are always going to let the patron have their way and set the pace of your library, why bother to have rules and policies in the first place? The patron is not always right.

A tough branch needs a tough manager and that is the bottom line. Someone with no leadership or management skills, just a love of books alone, is not going to be able to step up and do what needs to be done with any kind of consistency. I have seen this first hand over the years. Change to a more effective branch manager and see the various behavior problems miraculously become more controllable.

You also have to have the right managers and front line staff in those problematic departments. Why work in a branch that has a lot of teens coming in after school if you are afraid of them or have some bias against them (see the teen question in a few pages)?

Another problem I sometimes see in my travels is that some libraries have so much internal strife going on, it's impossible for managers to agree on anything, much less security procedures. This is where the strong manager has to step in and tell them what the ultimate decisions concerning procedures are going to be.

I was asked by a good friend in a library recently if I thought management and leadership were the same thing. After we shared a laugh over this question being a somewhat typical one in the library world, I answered that yes, of course they were. The best managers I have ever known truly managed staff and they led by example.

Question: *"How do you handle those rowdy teenagers?"*

Ah yes, the teen question. I am asked this so very often. This seems to be a growing problem in libraries, but I think the strategy for effectively dealing with it is pretty straight forward. I am hardly a child psychologist, and certainly not a teen librarian, but I have had a good amount of front line experience with kids. I also have the advantage of having traveled to almost every state and seen how libraries of all sizes in all different areas try to attract and serve teens.

I feel that I should remind you that most kids are good kids, despite what the media tries to tell you practically every day. Listen to the news long enough and you would think that all the young people who visit your branch are plotting to shoot up the school or are just thugs. Library staff often lament that kids just "aren't raised right" anymore, as if the new generation must be clones of our personalities to be correct. The plain fact is that many library staff are afraid of the kids simply because they often are so different that they are or were growing up.

First of all, let's remember that everyone must abide by the rules of your library and that includes the teens. Yes, I know we want them to come to the library. Yes, I know we want to be a "destination of choice" for these young people. Yes, I know we want to show them that we can give them the knowledge of the world and that it's all at their fingertips. But you cannot let them act anyway they want just so you can have a full teen area and a high usage rate on your computers. Some kids only understand the hard line and if they will not comply with the library rules, they can and should be ejected like anyone else. If you do not deny access to the kids who visit you for all the wrong reasons, then the students who honestly want to use the library for reading and studying will stop coming, thus you deny access to *them*.

The teen areas I have seen that are most successful are the ones that are adequately supervised. It is not a matter of not trusting the teens, but one of real world necessity. If your a teen center is a place where kids can be there alone and do anything they want, you will more than likely have problems.

I know I have made this point in answering a previous question, but it bears repeating and expansion. You have to have the right managers and staff in a library with high teen usage. I have seen great changes in young peoples' behavior in library branches once the manager changed. Not only do you need a strong leader who will be pro-active and assertive, but that manager also needs assistants who are on the same page. Inconsistency can kill your efforts to obtain and maintain a peaceful library environment.

The front line staff must be able to handle teens as well, and everyone must *like and enjoy* young people. How can you work in a library that is located right across the street from a school and not like kids? I see that situation often and if you have the wrong team with the wrong mindset they will not be able to communicate with those kids. They must not be afraid of them, and should get a sense of efficacy in helping them with their myriad of school work problems.

I remember visiting a library that I was told had a lot of kids who "were just out of control." I entered the building right after school had let out and there was indeed a sea of loud young patrons. It fascinated me that the staff members were all behind various desks or in the stacks, trying their best to ignore what was going on. It didn't take long for me to see that there was a "staff against teens" mentality, thus their progress was dead in the water.

We have to remember the tremendous social pressures that kids are subjected to these days. There is so much information available to them today, especially with the internet, and so many kids believe everything they read on the web. Don't you remember how tough it was to discover your identity? Think of what a teen goes through now with exposure to so much information and being so young.

We often forget how insecure some of us were and how we thought we had to cover up those feelings by posturing a certain way. Looking back I know that many of the silly things I did as a kid resulted from not feeling quite good enough. Many of the library staff I know would do themselves a favor by giving the whole issue of teens a little thought rather than automatically dismissing and pre-judging them when they come in the door.

Many libraries I observe could help themselves with the after school, student rush by simply limiting access to certain programs on certain computers during specific times. Before some of my librarian friends cringe and close the book, let me emphasize that I am not talking about "censorship," only managing your limited resources.

Let's say you have 20 computers in your library. The school bell rings and you become inundated with teens. They take over every available computer and while some are doing school work, others are turning your computer area into a video arcade. Then you have other groups hooting it up as they gather to look at MySpace or similar sites.

What is wrong with establishing, during peak use times, only four of those computers for gaming? Another four could be used for MySpace and chatting. Then you keep the other 12 for research and school work. This would give both the students who are in the library for their homework and research products, as well as *adults* who need to use a computer, fair accessibility to your limited computer resources.

If you have teen staff who can help control the use of the computers, then you probably don't have to consider this segmented approach (and I know some of my teen librarian friends are shuddering at this idea), but many smaller libraries do not have that type of staffing, so they have to use other measures to control the environment.

Another matter I think you should consider is making your teen area proportional to your overall square footage. Several times I have seen libraries trying to do too much with too little space and it causes problems. A large teen area in a very small branch can overwhelm the rest of the library, and your other patrons.

The layout of your building makes a difference also. If you basically have a large room divided into areas by the collection and not walls, a loud, unsupervised teen area can disrupt other areas of the library I have seen this in smaller libraries where the teens could be heard throughout the entire building.

Question: *"How should a staff member deal with a patron who wants to be too friendly?"*

Tell them that you are just too busy to listen to anything other than library business. Everybody has a different way of saying such things, but the point is that you usually have to tell them directly. I would add that you know they don't realize that they are being unreasonable with your time, but you have work to do.

I have seen patrons become infatuated with staff members who take the time to pay attention to them, however briefly.

Some of the people who come into the library are just lonely, I suppose.

If you aren't comfortable speaking directly to the patron, ask a co-worker or your supervisor for help. They can approach the person by saying, "I need to talk to you about a situation, and I know that you didn't mean anything, but you are making (staff name) a little uncomfortable. She didn't know how to tell you and she didn't want to hurt your feelings so that's why I'm giving you a head's up. Just keep some distance and let her do her work, OK?"

Question: *"How do you determine who to ban and how do you keep up with them?"*

Well, first of all, who wants to have to ban someone? Not I, and that was never the case, even though someone I worked with once said that "Warren just loves to ban people." I honestly never thought of that when I went into a security situation. I never wanted trouble or possible trouble and that is why I worked so hard to develop simple and effective procedures to perform my job with as little consternation on anyone's part as possible.

Having said that, there were plenty of patrons who simply got *themselves* banned. What are you to do after all? A patron will not comply with the rules of the library despite your best efforts. Do they get a pass, because nothing you say or do works with them?

Who on earth comes to the library drunk or whacked out on drugs? Who would think that a library is a place to go and wash both their clothes as well as themselves (and throw in a shave, too)? Who comes to a library to stalk women or try to touch them or just glare at them all day?

And how does one get banned from a library anyway? It always amazed me that people could not or would not control themselves in a library setting, especially when they later told me they had nowhere else to go. Many said that they were even banned from the local homeless facilities!

Which brings up another point: If shelters ban their patrons for not adhering to their rules and schools and community centers suspend kids for disallowed behavior, why would any library think they have to put up with disruptive behavior?

So, you have someone who will not go along with the simple, reasonable rules of the library and refuses to leave when asked. That is another example of the "out of control" behavior I discussed in my first book and that person should be ejected and banned.

It is truly fascinating to me that so many libraries have such extensive policies regarding zero tolerance for internal workplace problems, yet many excuse patrons, no matter how belligerent or aggressive they are to staff members.

Here is a simple log to use for simple reference of those who are not allowed back in your library. You can modify this form any way you need to, but you get the idea. You have a sheet for every letter of the alphabet and enter names last name first.

If you don't have a name, you can enter some nickname to know them by, but as in the potential problem log, make sure the moniker does not show bias.

The report number is the number from the original incident report you filled out when the person was banned. This provides easy reference if you need to review the entire report.

You will notice that in the last column you can enter the police report number if applicable. You could also add another column for the length of the ban if your library has several different ban periods.

TRESPASS LOG   LAST NAME BEGINS WITH ___ D ___

Name	Race	Sex	Date of Warning	Security Officer	Police Officer	Incident Number	Picture	Problem	Police Report Number
John Doe	W	M	4.29.09	Smith	Lee	001-10	Yes	Intox	7382

Question: *"How did you handle the banning process and could a banned patron file an appeal of some type?"*

Yes, there should be a process to appeal a ban. I required the patron to write a letter to the director of the library, who would then go over the details of the security situation with me. Based on what had originally happened, we then decided if we though we could give the patron another chance.

However, if someone had committed some sexual offense, communicated a threat or actually assaulted staff or patrons, I always voted to not let them return. Some would say that you are inviting a lawsuit if you deny access permanently, but if their offense is extreme enough, I think you are better off keeping them out. After all, who would you rather have sue you, the screwball who can't even come into a library without exposing himself, or the family of a young child who was his victim after you allowed a known pervert back in your building?

Question: *"What if I have to call the police to help eject a patron or arrest them for trespass and they leave before the police arrive?"*

First, make sure you form a good relationship with the police. Meet with them and show them you have clear procedures to handle security situations that occur in libraries. Tell them that staff is trained and that the police are never called unless there is an emergency. Develop a contact with the police department with whom you can follow up if you have any problems with response time.

Make sure you thoroughly document everything in your security report, including the time the police were called and the name of the officer and time they responded. Be sure to do this whether the patron leaves before the police arrive or not.

If the subject does leave before officers get there and then eventually returns, I would try to stay as low key as possible and call the police. If you have your documentation from the previous incident, you can ban the person based on what previously occurred. The important thing to remember is that you do not have to wait for the subject to do something else to ban them upon their return to your library.

If you were able to tell the patron that he was banned during the original incident, he could be arrested for trespass when he returns, but the police may want to give the subject another chance by warning him – in their presence – against returning in to the library.

Of course, all of this will vary based on exactly who is authorized to tell someone they cannot return at your library, but the overall process is basically the same.

Question: *"What if we are accused of some type of bias by someone we ban?"*

You will be accused of bias sooner or later, as I often was. Ninety-nine percent of the time, it's just a way for the behavior problem to try to distract you from the real issues at hand. I never even responded to such accusations, and here is why.

You must be sure you are consistent with your banning process, and that you treat everyone the same. I have seen people from all walks of life commit crimes and/or do incredibly bizarre things. Would that it were that we could always predict who the bad guy is going to be.

Naturally, if you have a lot of problems with people who appear homeless, you are going to notice the individual who walks in looking like they slept under a bridge all night over the person dressed in a business suit. That is just being human and it is not profiling. Profiling is when you make assumptions and do not give the person the benefit of a doubt and pre-judge him.

I certainly have approached some of the best dressed and well-groomed people to tell them they could not do something and have been met with serious aggression. Conversely, I have spoken to some of the roughest looking folks who were the most compliant. If you pre-judge, you make your job harder, so don't do it. Take each individual as they come, based on behavior and never appearance

Having rules is not a problem, but if you pick and choose who to enforce the rules with, that will get you in trouble quickly. Treat everyone the same and you won't have to work in fear of accusations of bias.

Question: *"Do we need a camera system in our library?"*

I changed my opinion on this recently, having traveled and seen so many different types of library designs. I am now of the opinion that yes, most libraries need some type of a camera system, a basic one at the very least. What I mean by basic is camera locations that are shooting patrons both entering and leaving the library, showing them at the angles and with the clarity to identify them if needed.

This way, if you ban someone, you don't have to worry about getting a picture. With good, well placed cameras and a VCR, it is a simple matter to review the "history" of the data and print a photo from the monitor screen.

This set-up will also be of vital importance if a child is ever taken from the library, so <u>all managers</u> need to know how to work the VCR properly and expediently.

Of course, some libraries need more extensive camera positioning. Fortunately, with technology advancing the way it always is, the costs of these systems are coming down all the time. Be sure to get two or three vendors to come in a bid against one another, but don't sacrifice quality for the low bid. You get what you pay for.

And while we are talking about cameras, forget about "dummy" camera locations. It does not cost that much more to get the real thing, and you do not want to promote a false sense of security.

Are cameras an "invasion of privacy," as a seminar attendee recently asked me? Of course not. You're not sitting around a panel of monitors zooming in trying to see what a patron is reading. Your cameras are there for everyone's safety. You are also showing that you are attempting to be good stewards of the public's property, i.e. the books and materials, by using cameras to help prevent mutilation or theft. Most patrons, times being what they are, expect to see reasonable security measures in place.

The first couple of years at the library, patrons would occasionally stop me and ask who I was and why did the library need its own security. Soon after, they stopped asking me since they grew accustomed to seeing security practically every where they went.

Part Four:
Real World Security Staffing

"Is there anyone so wise as to learn from the past?"
—Voltaire

Question: *"Do you recommend contract or in-house security?"*

Even at the library in Charlotte, the county periodically raised subject of contract security in an effort to cut every penny that they possibly could. This always amazed me since the repeated and total failure of several contract security companies is what directly led to my being hired and initiating a proprietary security staff!

It has been my experience that contractual security firms rarely work out. Am I saying that none of those guards know what they are doing? No, of course not; I hired my assistant in Charlotte when all he had was contract company experience. But, from all that I have seen and heard, dealing with the various consequences of going that route is, more often than not, problematic at best.

Hiring your own security staff can be difficult enough. Good help is hard to find, as the old saying goes and that is even more true when it comes to security personnel, but that doesn't mean you can't find it. If they are your own staff, you have infinitely more control over them. With your own staff, you know exactly how they were trained. You know about their backgrounds and personalities because you interviewed them and hired them. You have immediate authority to correct any shortcomings, to write them up or even terminate them.

Your staff will usually care much more about the facility than a contracted employee. To many contract staff, your library is just another gig and it is rare to find someone that will go the extra mile and "step up" in difficult situations like your own hire would.

Question: *"How do you uniform security officers?"*

I would yet again stress simplicity. I always clothed my staff with plain black slacks and blue polo shirts that had the library logo on the front with "Security" added. I also provided jackets and caps with the same logo. They wore a North Carolina Security Officer badge in a clip holder on the right front of their belt. They carried handcuffs only; no pepper spray or baton or any other weapon. I wanted their "weapons" to be their minds. I wanted them to use their wits rather than automatically falling back on some weapon. This was in our particular security environment. There may be times when weapons are justified, such as in a multiple building setting, with late night patrols, etc.

I had worked in positions where I wore a more classic "guard" uniform. I found that most experienced behavior problems thought I was the typical guard from a contract service, thus they assumed I was ill-trained and unsure and they often tried to take advantage of that assumption. I didn't want my staff to be underestimated in any way, so I uniformed them much differently. Indeed, I've seen uniforms that were taken to their logical absurdity, with a myriad of patches, whistles, broad rimmed hats with badges atop and the like, so much so they looked as if they were in a costume like one of the Village People!

Now I have seen formal, classic style uniforms that could work, that are extremely close to police uniforms with custom patches (rather than the generic "Security Officer" patch you can get from any internet source) and badges. Even then, you want to keep the accessories to a minimum. The uniforms also need to actually fit the officer. Nothing looks worse than a uniform just off the rack and two sizes too big.

I learned by utilizing different uniforms that subtle or "soft" was better. While there are some exceptions, generally I prefer polo's with the library logo and "Security" embroidered on the front with black slacks, shoes and socks. I wore athletic shoes and certainly allowed my staff to do the same, but they had to be solid black ones; no color stripes or insignias, etc. I supplied the uniforms, but it was up to the officer to always keep them cleaned and pressed.

Some have questioned why my officers had handcuffs and the reason was simple. Sooner or later your officers will have to put their hands on someone. That, in turn, usually leads to the behavior problem being restrained in handcuffs. Proper handcuff techniques have saved me and patrons from serious injury.

And speaking of your officers defending themselves or others, you'd better arrange for proper training of defensive techniques. You can theorize that your library doesn't want the officer to have to touch someone all you want, but if you are in a problematic library, sooner or later they will have to. That is just the way it is. Some behavior problems only understand the hard line and you do not want the officer to be so vulnerable. Keep in mind also that you will document his training in these techniques so if the officer ever goes farther than necessary, you have proof of how he was properly trained. This will help if you ever face litigation.

I stated in my previous book that officers should be in good shape. This has always been a tick of mine as a security manager. Mind you, I am not talking about someone looking like the cover of a fitness magazine; they should just be able to move quickly and adequately come to your aid without having problems due to a lack of fitness. Can they go up the steps to help you or do they need to wait on the elevator?

This also goes along with my opinion that officers should be standing and moving around most of the time and not sitting, which requires reasonable fitness.

Question: *"What attributes do security officers need and how should they be trained?"*

They must be well-groomed and always "on task." You want an "officer" and not a "guard." You want a professional, well trained and objective individual that readily gives the public the benefit of the doubt and resolves incidents in the library's best interest.

A security officer must be someone you can trust to do the job, being visible and vigilant even when the manager isn't around. A strong work ethic and sense of responsibility is absolutely critical. I always told my security staff that the library could not function properly without us, and I meant that.

In my first book I talked about how vital consistency amongst staff is when it comes to security matters. That goes even more so for security officers. They must function as a unit and all follow the same procedures day in and day out. If you have an officer who is more stringent with banning, or notably less so than the other security staff, he could be accused of some type of bias.

Officers have to get past the barrier of the badge. Many people may come into your library who resent authority, and when they see your officer, they are going to have a chip on their shoulder. It takes a talent to be able to stay relaxed and flow with a situation that involves a behavior problem who throws everything your officer says back in his face.

He/she must be able to have the ability to communicate a negative in the most positive way possible. I cannot emphasize this point enough. You can not train your staff to have a sincere interest in and empathy with patrons; the officer must bring that to the job.

Question: *"How and when should front line staff interact with the security officer?"*

Folks often ask me when they should call security and I always say whenever you are in doubt of a situation, whether it is overt or just something you suspect, certainly call your officer. If the situation turns out to be nothing or a minor interaction, well, that's good. Security should never chastise a staff member for calling them.

Please remember that just because you have security doesn't mean you can stick your head back in the sand and forget about your day-to-day security responsibilities. Your security officer can't be everywhere all the time no matter how much he walks around. Officers depend on staff to let them know about suspicious behavior as well as overt acts.

Nothing would get on my nerves more than when after with a behavior problem, an employee would comment to me that the person had been acting questionably for a while! Why didn't the staff member give me a heads up? I was only a phone call away. I never understood that.

Should you always call security every time someone breaks a rule? Of course not. You can embarrass a patron to the point of a verbal confrontation. Do you really need a person with a badge to tell a patron that they can't have a soda by the computer every time you see it happen?

Staff need to understand and remember that security personnel are there to *augment* their own awareness and security efforts, not to take the place of them. Staff cannot afford to stop paying attention to their environment just because they have security in the building.

Also, your officers need to move around on a timely basis. This means no hanging out behind the reference or other public service desk or engaging in prolonged conversations with other staff. Again, they must always stay both visible and vigilant and you can't do that while sitting somewhere doing a crossword puzzle!

Question: *"What if a contract officer does not perform to our standards?"*

Never hesitate to demand his replacement, period. You are paying for a service and if the officer does not meet your requirements, the company must expediently respond to your concern. The officer is there to prevent and solve problems; not to be one. Do not allow a poor return on your investment. Monitor them when they work for you and make sure they are doing what you need them to do. Don't assume they have the same feeling of responsibility for your library that you do.

The security company you use/hire needs to know from the start that you will execute this plan when you are not satisfied with performance. Give the company a list of expectations for their employees, so they will know what to expect when they work for you. Keep the responsibility for professionalism with the company and never pay for sub-standard service.

In Closing

There you have them. The most frequently asked questions from my training sessions. I'm grateful for the chance to give you some further guidelines to help control the atmosphere of the library.

I will leave you with questions of my own that I often asked my friends in the library world. How would *you* answer them?

1—Why do we *really* say that libraries aren't quiet places anymore? How often is that statement actually based on more patrons, computers, etc. versus many library staff's apprehensions when it comes to correcting behavior? Is it easier to say that the library is "just noisier these days" than it is to approach and tell a patron to lower his/her voice?

2—Would we rather say that the public is just "getting worse" when it comes to their behavior rather than doing the work to educate them as to what is not allowed in the library? Are you going to give up or are you and your co-workers going to commit to control your library's environment?

3—Why is the issue of patron behavior such a hot topic today? Is it because the library's traditionally passive approaches just aren't working? Is it time to hold the patrons responsible for their behavior? You are a professional and deserve to be treated in a civil manner by the public. Is that really too much to ask? Shouldn't the responsibility for patrons' behavior rest with them?

4—Why do all complaints about patron behavior that result in action have to come from other patrons? Don't the opinions of staff mean anything at all? Can't staff observe and report?

5—When you say that you "don't want to be a police officer," is that just another way of avoiding telling a patron "no?"

6—Are you going to have a plan for security situations or are you just going to open and hope nothing happens tomorrow morning? Are you just continuing the gambling approach of rolling the dice and seeing what comes up? That is a terrible game you are playing with your safety.

7—Whatever your existing policy is, does it help or hinder you? Are you in control of the library environment or is the patron?

8—How serious are you about your security? I mean, are you really committed to controlling your library's environment? Does your administration know what they want and are they leading the implementation of the plan?

Here is the thing to remember: any library environment can be controlled, and that includes yours. Robert Cannon and I proved that in Charlotte. It can be done and is done in many libraries that I have visited.

Of course, I am not saying that my way is the only way, but it is indeed a real-world, proven way. *From the concept of library security to an actual functioning plan that works is a huge gap.* It is my sincere wish I have helped you narrow and close that gap.

I wish you all the best with your security efforts and hope to visit your library someday.

About the Author

A security professional for over 25 years, spending 17 as the security manager of the Public Library of Charlotte and Mecklenburg County, Warren Graham left the library in August of 2006 to establish Warren Davis Graham Training and Consulting. Warren has made countless presentations and is internationally considered to be the leading speaker on practical day-to-day library security procedures. Warren is also the author of the best selling *Black Belt Librarians: Every Librarian's Real World Guide to a Safer Workplace.* His next book will be *Real Self-Defense for Librarians: Easy and Simple Techniques for Everyone.*

Contact Warren can for training and consulting through his website:

www.BlackBeltLibrarians.com